IMAGES OF SINGAPORE

Marshall Cavendish
Editions

© 2011 Marshall Cavendish International (Asia) Private Limited

Published by Marshall Cavendish Editions
An imprint of Marshall Cavendish International
1 New Industrial Road, Singapore 536196

Design & Photographs: Bernard Go Kwang Meng
Text: Stephanie Yeo

Other Marshall Cavendish Offices:
Marshall Cavendish International. PO Box 65829, London EC1P 1NY, UK • Marshall Cavendish Corporation. 99 White Plains Road, Tarrytown NY 10591-9001, USA • Marshall Cavendish International (Thailand) Co Ltd. 253 Asoke, 12th Flr, Sukhumvit 21 Road, Klongtoey Nua, Wattana, Bangkok 10110, Thailand • Marshall Cavendish (Malaysia) Sdn Bhd, Times Subang, Lot 46, Subang Hi-Tech Industrial Park, Batu Tiga, 40000 Shah Alam, Selangor Darul Ehsan, Malaysia.

Marshall Cavendish is a trademark of Times Publishing Limited

National Library Board, Singapore Cataloguing-in-Publication Data

Images of Singapore. – Singapore : Marshall Cavendish Editions, c2011.
p. cm.
ISBN : 978-981-4328-65-4 (pbk.)
1. Photography, Artistic. 2. Singapore – Pictorial works.
DS609.2
779.995957 — dc22   OCN698537849

Printed in Singapore by Fabulous Printers Pte Ltd

00 IMAGES

CONTENTS

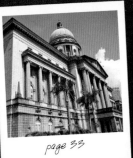

01

INTRODUCTION

From its humble beginnings as a small fishing village and later a key trading port in Southeast Asia, Singapore today straddles the unique divide between modernity and tradition, with one of the world's fastest rates of economic growth.

NATIONAL DAY

Previously a British colony and later part of the Federation of Malaysia, Singapore officially gained independence on 9 August 1965. The momentous occasion is commemorated annually with an exuberant National Day Parade.

Spectators dress in red and white – the nation's colours – at the annual National Day Parade.

Military displays by the Singapore Armed Forces are a perennial parade highlight.

NATIONAL FLOWER

The Vanda Miss Joachim was chosen as Singapore's national flower in 1981. The lovely purple orchid was selected for its hardy resilient qualities and ability to bloom throughout the year.

NATIONAL FLAG

The national flag of Singapore was first adopted in 1965. It comprises two equal horizontal sections of red (on top) and white (below); red representing universal brotherhood while white symbolises everlasting purity and virtue. The white crescent moon represents a young nation, and the five stars symbolise the nation's ideals: democracy, peace, progress, justice and equality.

02

A multicultural kaleidoscope of immigrants from the region, Singapore's cosmopolitan society comprises five main ethnic groups – Chinese, Malays, Indians, Peranakans and Eurasians. Each community's rich heritage and cultural values are deeply ingrained into the fabric of Singapore's past and present.

PEOPLE & CULTURE

CHINESE

Comprising almost three-quarters of the population, ethnic Chinese in Singapore are made up of many dialect groups, such as Hokkien, Cantonese, Teochew and Hakka. Each has its own language, although most speak Mandarin as a common platform for conversation.

CHINESE NEW YEAR

Chinese New Year is one of the most celebrated festivals in the Chinese calendar. Extended families gather on the eve of Chinese New Year for a reunion dinner. Traditionally, red packets (or *hong bao*) containing money are given to younger members of the family for good luck.

The festivities are especially palpable in Chinatown, where the streets are decorated in red (signifying good luck), and the smells of *bak kwa* (barbecued pork) and other traditional snacks and Chinese New Year tunes fill the air. Spicing up the festivities during this 15-day celebration are the River Hong Bao Carnival and Chingay Parade.

Symbolising riches and good fortune, mandarin oranges are an auspicious Chinese New Year fruit.

MID-AUTUMN FESTIVAL

Also known as the Mooncake or Lantern Festival, the Mid-Autumn Festival usually falls in August. Families and friends give each another mooncakes, which are delicious pastries filled with a variety of ingredients ranging from lotus paste to white chocolate.

Chinatown is a swirl of activity, its streets beautifully lit with dazzling lantern displays. Many events are organised all over Singapore in celebration of this festival, such as lantern installations, special performances and demonstrations.

MALAY

The Malays are the nation's original inhabitants and the second largest ethnic group in Singapore. This warm and hospitable community traces its ancestry to the Bugis from Sulawesi, the Boyanese from Madura in Indonesia and the Orang Laut, who are descendants of the Sea Gypsies.

HARI RAYA PUASA

Hari Raya Puasa is celebrated after the Islamic fasting month (Ramadan). During this festival, Muslims dress in traditional ethnic clothing, children receive money in green packets (*duit raya*) and younger Muslims seek forgiveness from their elders for any misdeeds.

The districts of Geylang Serai and Kampong Glam are usually abuzz with street performances and light-ups, as well as numerous bazaars selling all sorts of delectable Malay snacks and treats.

INDIAN

The smallest of the three major ethnic groups, the Indians were originally immigrants who arrived in Singapore to work and provide for their families back home. Over time, they brought their families with them and settled down permanently. The community is a tight-knit one, and still practices many traditions and customs from the Indian subcontinent.

DEEPAVALI

Deepavali is also known as the Festival of Lights and celebrates Lord Krishna's victory over the demon of darkness. Hindus commemorate the triumph of good over evil by lighting oil lamps. They also wear new clothes to mark the occasion and family and friends visit one another.

Little India in the Serangoon area is an explosion of the senses during Deepavali. Shops selling garlands, oil lamps and gorgeous saris line the streets alongside stalls hawking all sorts of delicious food. Festive lights adorn the roads and trees, adding to the electrifying atmosphere.

THAIPUSAM

One of the most amazing festivals in Singapore, Thaipusam is not for the faint hearted. In a show of devotion and gratitude to Lord Murugan, devotees carry a *kavadi*, a heavy steel framework that is anchored to their bare bodies. Devotees also pierce their tongue, cheeks, lips and other body parts with skewers, spikes and other similar sharp objects. They then walk barefoot for about 4 km. Other believers join in the procession, carrying milk jars in offering to Lord Murugan.

PERANAKAN

Many of the early Chinese immigrants to Malaya and Singapore married Malay women, giving birth to a community of people known as the Peranakans (which means "locally born"). Also known as Straits Chinese or Straits-born Chinese, the Peranakans pride themselves on their unique culture and cuisine, which has evolved and developed over the centuries.

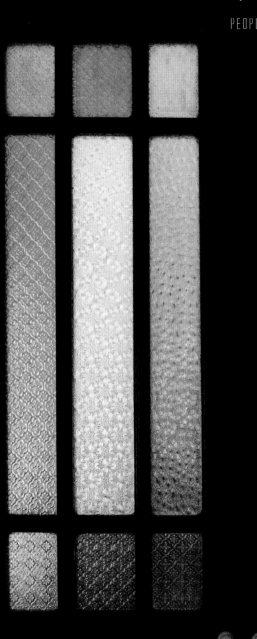

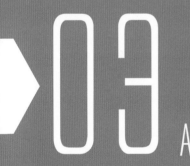

03 ARCHITECTURAL ICONS

Gleaming, modern skyscrapers sit amongst
charming colonial architecture and busy wet markets
in Singapore – a dynamic architectural mix of old
and new, East and West, and past and present.

RAFFLES HOTEL

Named after Sir Stamford Raffles, the founder of Singapore, the Raffles Hotel is a luxurious colonial-style hotel dating back to 1887. An oasis of lush tropical gardens in the heart of the city, the hotel is renowned for its elegant French Renaissance architecture and impeccable service.

STAMFORD RAFFLES STATUE

There are two statues of Sir Stamford Raffles – one in front of the Victoria Theatre and Concert Hall at Empress Place and another at the bank of the Singapore River. The original bronze statue was inaugurated in 1887 at the Padang, before being moved to its present location in 1919. A white marble replica of this statue was placed at the mouth of the Singapore River, marking Raffles' landing site when he first set foot in Singapore in 1819.

VICTORIA THEATRE
AND CONCERT HALL

Originally built as a memorial
to Queen Victoria, the Victoria
Theatre and Concert Hall is
today a popular performance
and entertainment venue.

The construction of the signature
four-faced clock tower, which
rises to a height of 54 metres,
was completed in 1906.

ISTANA

Reminiscent of neo-Palladian style buildings in the 18th century, the Istana is Singapore's equivalent of the White House and the official residence of the president of Singapore. Originally built in 1867 as the home of Singapore's first colonial governor, the Istana – which means "palace" in Malay – is where the president receives and entertains state guests.

MERLION

An iconic symbol of Singapore, the Merlion is a mythical creature with the head of a lion and the body of a mermaid. Originally constructed at the mouth of the Singapore River, the majestic Merlion statue now stands in front of One Fullerton at Marina Bay.

CHANGI AIRPORT

With more than 350 accolades under its belt – including "Best Airport in the World" by *Business Traveller* (UK) for 22 consecutive years – Changi International Airport has come a long way since its humble beginnings in 1981. Now the sixth busiest international airport in the world, Changi Airport has four passenger terminals, including the state-of-the-art Terminal 3 that opened in 2008. Visitors can enjoy a vast array of amenities and services, including foot reflexology, a leisurely stroll in the Butterfly Garden and a refreshing dip in the rooftop swimming pool.

Conveniently located next to Terminal 3, the Crowne Plaza Changi Airport hotel is a work of art with its dramatic latticework of tropical flowers.

OLD SUPREME COURT BUILDING

The last Neoclassical building to be built in Singapore, the former courthouse of the Supreme Court of Singapore was constructed between 1937–39 in front of the historical Padang grounds. Buried beneath the landmark building's foundation stone is a time capsule containing six Singaporean newspapers dated 31 March 1937 and some Straits Settlement coins – scheduled for retrieval only in the year 3000.

OLD PARLIAMENT HOUSE

A grandiose Victorian structure, the Old Parliament House was designed and built by Singapore's colonial architect, George Coleman, in 1827. The historic building was converted into an arts and heritage venue in 2004 and relaunched as The Arts House, which hosts films, art exhibitions, plays and musical concerts. Taking pride of place outside the building is a majestic bronze elephant, a gift from King Rama V of Thailand in 1871.

MICA BUILDING

With its brightly-hued wooden window shutters, the MICA Building is an unmistakable splash of colour in Clarke Quay. A gazetted national monument since 1998, the six-storey building was formerly the Hill Street Police Station, and one of the tallest and most modern buildings back in 1934. The Neoclassical style building has since been restored and given a new lease of life as the home of the Ministry of Information, Communication and the Arts.

THE FULLERTON HOTEL

Built in 1928 and named after Robert Fullerton, the first Governor of the Straits Settlements, the Fullerton Building used to house the General Post Office, the Chamber of Commerce and The Singapore Club. Once an important trade and economic centre, this magnificent Neoclassical colonial building is now the luxurious Fullerton Hotel overlooking the Singapore River.

ESPLANADE
THEATRES ON THE BAY

Singapore's epicentre of the arts, the Esplanade is one of the world's busiest performing arts centres – home to a grand concert hall, outdoor theatre, recital and theatre studio, as well as numerous restaurants and specialty cafes.

Strategically located by the Marina Bay waterfront, the Esplanade is dubbed the "durian" because of its unique louvered roof, which bears a resemblance to the pungent, thorny fruit of the Southeast Asian region.

SRI MARIAMMAN TEMPLE

Singapore's oldest Hindu temple, the Sri Mariamman temple, is rather surprisingly located in the heart of Chinatown. The landmark temple has tiers of various gods and deities from Hindu mythology carved on its main structure, and remains a key focal point of the Indian community.

SULTAN MOSQUE

Originally built between 1824–26 by Sultan Hussain Shah, the first sultan of Singapore, the Sultan Mosque is a regal arabesque structure replete with domes, minarets and balustrades.
To accomodate the growing Muslim community, a bigger mosque was built on the same site at North Bridge Road between 1924–26. It is now a gazetted national monument.

THIAN HOCK KENG TEMPLE

Built on the site of a popular joss house at Telok Ayer Street, the Thian Hock Keng Temple is one of Singapore's oldest Chinese temples. The richly-ornamented building has curved roofs and sharp edges decorated with animals from mythical Chinese folklore. Following a major restoration, the landmark temple was awarded the UNESCO Asia-Pacific Heritage Conservation Award in 2001.

ST. ANDREW'S CATHEDRAL

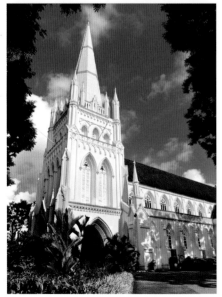

The first and largest Anglican Church in Singapore, St. Andrew's Cathedral was built in 1857 by Colonel Ronald McPherson of the Madras army. With its extended pinnacles, arched entrance and glossy white exterior, the majestic neo-Gothic styled building was gazetted as a national monument in 1973, and is one of Singapore's most treasured works of architecture.

GOODWOOD PARK HOTEL

Formerly known as the Teutonia Club, which served the Germany expatriate community in Singapore during its colonial years, the Goodwood Park Hotel was built in 1900 and declared a national monument in 1989. The South German architecture features ornamental works and a large semi-circular gable end flanking the entrance.

CHIJMES

Formerly a Catholic girls school and convent (Convent of the Holy Infant Jesus) in the mid-19th century, CHIJMES was the seat of education for generations of Singapore girls until it closed its doors in 1983. Retaining its magical, old-world charm, the neo-Gothic style building has since been restored and is now a popular retail, dining and entertainment venue.

PUBLIC HOUSING

Many Singaporeans live in high-rise HDB (Housing Development Board) flats, which are located in public housing estates with amenities such as hawker centres, shops, medical clinics and recreational facilities within walking distance.

The nation's progressive economic development is reflected in the changing face of its public housing, from the quaint structures of yesteryear to the gleaming facades of the Pinnacle@Duxton *(right)*.

KLAPSONS THE BOUTIQUE HOTEL

Stunning architecture meets modern functionality at Klapsons, a boutique hotel located in the heart of Singapore's vibrant business district. Guests are received in a spherical lobby adorned with avant garde furniture and art, a prelude to the luxurious suites where goose down pillows, Egyptian cotton sheets and sophisticated designer pieces complete the experience.

CAPELLA SINGAPORE

A tranquil oasis away from the city's bustle, Capella's peaceful setting atop a knoll spans 30 acres of lush rainforest on Sentosa Island, with breathtaking views of the South China Sea. Built in the 1880s by the British Military, two regal colonial buildings form the heart of the luxurious resort; masterfully restored in a harmonious blend of old-world architecture with modern design and sculpture gardens rich with contemporary art.

WANDERLUST

Nestled in the heart of Little India, a bustling cultural enclave where Indian immigrants once reared cattle and livestock, Wanderlust began its history as an old school in the 1920s. Opened in 2010, this quirky four-storey boutique hotel features the groundbreaking work of award-winning Singapore designers in each of its 29 unique rooms, blending contemporary art nouveau with the rustic old-world charm of its restored facade.

04 LOCALES

From the ultramodern business district to authentic cultural enclaves bursting with exotic sights, scents and smells, the Little Red Dot is home to a diverse spectrum of exciting locales.

CENTRAL BUSINESS DISTRICT

The heart of Singapore's financial hub, the Central Business District includes core financial and commercial areas such as Marina Bay, Raffles Place and Shenton Way. Big international names jostle cheek to cheek with local ones in towering skyscrapers overlooking the Singapore River, alongside the important cultural heritage areas of Chinatown and Tanjong Pagar.

LITTLE INDIA

Once the locale of the original Tamil migrants, Little India is today a bustling enclave of traditional shophouses and colourful shops interspersed with temples. A treasure trove for the senses, the district offers everything from olden-day fortune-telling and delicate saris to the heady scents of jasmine garlands, exotic spices and delicious Indian delicacies.

CHINATOWN

A haven for all things *chinois*, Chinatown offers a fascinating peek into Singapore's rich Chinese culture and its history. Amidst beautifully restored ornate stucco shophouses, family-run goldsmith shops and colourful textile stores, food remains a strong presence here. Dim sum restaurants and genteel teahouses line the lanes and alleyways, and Smith Street, an alfresco paradise of local delicacies, is a popular haunt for locals and visitors alike.

GEYLANG SERAI

Leading up to the Muslim festive seasons, the precinct of Geylang Serai comes to life in a riot of colours, with night markets and stalls in the Malay Village selling everything from traditional costumes to festive goodies and intricate handicrafts. The recently renovated Geylang Serai Market, a two-storey complex filled with shops hawking fresh produce and ethnic clothing and trinkets, also offers some of the best Malay and Indian-Muslim dishes in Singapore.

Once the seat of the Malay royalty in Singapore, Kampong Glam has been an iconic Malay-Muslim precinct since the early 1800s. Awash with exotic smells, sights and sounds – from fragrant spices and traditional hand-woven carpets to modern art galleries and curios shops – the enclave's bustling alleyways are a treasure trove of art and culture to excite the senses.

KAMPONG GLAM

At the heart of Kampong Glam's vibrancy is the Sultan Mosque, one of Singapore's most prominent national monuments. The area was designated a heritage conservation area in 1989.

ARAB STREET

LAU PA SAT

Nestled amidst tall, gleaming skyscrapers in Shenton Way financial district is Telok Ayer Market, or Lau Pa Sat, a cast-iron Victorian-era building with an octagonal roof and a four-faced clock tower. A familiar landmark since 1894, the 24-hour market is home to a vast array of food stalls hawking local delicacies such as fragrant satay and barbecued seafood. The historic building was gazetted as a national monument in 1973.

CLARKE QUAY

A historical riverside quay situated at the mouth of the Singapore River, Clarke Quay was Singapore's epicentre of commerce in the late 19th century. Today, the bustling waterfront enclave pays homage to its heritage with a colourful kaleidoscope of restaurants, wine bars, entertainment spots and retail shops nestled amidst rows of charming shophouses, modern pushcarts and five-foot-way merchants.

ORCHARD ROAD

Deriving its name from the bountiful fruit orchards and plantations that used to span the area, Singapore's famed Orchard Road is the Little Red Dot's answer to Los Angeles' Rodeo Drive. Testament to its reputation as a shopping haven, the premier shopping belt is lined cheek to cheek with high-end shopping malls, luxury hotels and tourist attractions.

Previously the historic Killiney Post Office, KPO is today a vibrant two-storey bar bounded by Killiney, Penang and Orchard Road.

05 NATURE

Often celebrated as a cosmopolitan "Garden City", Singapore's cityscape is complemented by its thriving ecosystem of lush greenery, nature and wildlife. From the trees and flora lining the island to landscaped gardens and protected rainforests, Singapore's numerous green enclaves offer close commune with nature, even in the heart of the city.

A welcome respite from the bustle of the city, the Singapore Botanic Gardens encompass 64 hectares of verdant greenery, including sprawling lawns overlooking tranquil lakes, fountains and beautiful sculpture gardens. The resplendent on-site National Orchid Garden houses over 1,000 species and 2,000 hybrids of tropical orchids – the largest display of such in the world.

BOTANIC GARDENS

Bathe in the urban oasis of the Singapore Botanic Gardens — from leisurely evening strolls to a relaxing picnic on the lawn, this green sanctuary is the perfect place to recharge and rejuvenate.

SUNGEI BULOH WETLAND RESERVE

On the northwestern end of Singapore is a rare oasis, a thriving wetland of brackish and fresh-water ponds, mangrove mudflats, estuaries and swamps. Popular with nature and adventure enthusiasts, Sungei Buloh Wetland Reserve is home to a vast ecosystem of wildlife and lush flora and fauna, including kingfishers, mudskippers and, if you're lucky, a resident family of Smooth Otters and the rare Malayan water monitor.

MACRITCHIE RESERVOIR

One of Singapore's most popular nature parks, MacRitchie Reservoir is a protected water catchment reserve with over 3,000 hectares of surrounding rainforest. The many boardwalks and rugged walking trails provide an instant escape from the concrete jungle of the city, and the HSBC Treetop Walk *(right)*, a 250-metre aerial suspension bridge that spans the two highest points in MacRitchie, offers a panoramic bird's-eye view of the rainforest canopy.

SOUTHERN RIDGES

Combining several walking trails through the hills of Mount Faber Park, Telok Blangah Hill Park and Kent Ridge Park, the Southern Ridges is home to many of Mother Nature's greatest gifts, and the purveyor of some of the most spectacular views of the city. Popular trails include the Canopy, Hilltop and Forest Walks, as well as the undulating Henderson Waves *(below)*, the highest pedestrian bridge in Singapore.

PULAU UBIN

Discover what life was like in 1960s Singapore on Pulau Ubin, a small island northeast of Singapore and home of the last *kampong* (village) from bygone days. Meaning "Granite Island" in Malay, the island was once known for its numerous granite quarries that supplied the local construction industry. Today, Pulau Ubin is a popular getaway destination for cyclists and nature lovers.

Chek Jawa, an intertidal flat and one-time coral reef on the island, boasts a virtually untouched sanctuary of rich ecosystems and marine wildlife.

CHINESE GARDEN

Built in 1975 and designed by a renowned Taiwanese architect, the serene Chinese Garden is modelled after the northern Chinese imperial style of integrated landscaping and architecture. Enjoy a leisurely stroll amidst majestic pagodas, rainbow bridges and a gentle stream, and marvel at the beautiful Bonsai Garden, which features over a thousand bonsai trees from China.

BUKIT TIMAH NATURE RESERVE

Designated a protected reserve in 1883, Bukit Timah Nature Reserve
is the only substantial area of primary rainforest left in Singapore. The
163-hectare Nature Reserve includes Bukit Timah Hill, Singapore's highest
hill, and is home to one of the world's most diverse ecological systems. In
fact, the number of tree species growing in a mere hectare of the Reserve
is more than the total number of tree species in all of North America.

EAST COAST PARK

The largest park in Singapore, East Coast Park is built entirely on reclaimed land with a man-made beach protected by breakwaters. Its cool sea breezes and myriad of available recreational activities makes the beachside park a popular weekend family destination, with chalets and barbecue pits, bicycle and inline skate rental, and even wakeboarding facilities all within walking distance.

06 FOOD

Singaporean food is as exotic and varied as its peoples. From spicy Chinese cuisine and tantalising curries to wonderful breads and tasty nyonya goodies, the Republic's rich multicultural heritage offers a gourmet paradise that is certain to pique even the most discerning palates.

CHILLI CRAB

HAINANESE CHICKEN RICE

A dish best eaten using one's hands, chilli crab is a heady concoction of hard shell crabs seared in a rich, thick tomato, egg and chilli-based gravy. One of Singapore's favourite dishes, chilli crab is often eaten with *mantou*, delicious fried buns that help to soak up the remaining sauce.

Hainanese chicken rice is widely considered to be Singapore's national dish. Adapted to local tastes by Hainanese immigrants, the flavourful dish consists of fragrant rice cooked in chicken stock, topped with slices of steamed chicken and cucumber and accompanied by chilli sauce, ginger paste and dark soy sauce.

SATAY

ROTI PRATA

Delicious skewers of marinated meat – usually chicken, beef or lamb – grilled over charcoal, satay is traditionally served with slivers of raw onions, chewy *ketupat* (rice cake) slices, cucumber and a spicy peanut gravy.

A traditional Indian speciality, roti prata is a flaky flatbread pancake fried over a flat grill to give it its golden-brown colour. Usually served with a spicy curry gravy, popular variants include roti prata with cheese, egg, mushrooms and even bananas and chocolate.

CHAR KWAY TEOW

POPIAH

Another of Singapore's signature dishes, char kway teow is a fried flat rice noodle dish, often tossed with prawns, egg, cockles, bean sprouts and sweet, dark sauce. The secret of a good char kway teow lies in the quality of ingredients and skill in achieving "*wok hei*", the smoky flavour from a hot wok.

A fresh spring roll made from a soft, paper-like crepe, traditional popiah is filled with a variety of ingredients such as steamed turnip, bean sprouts, omelette strips, chopped peanuts and shrimp, together with a sweet sauce.

LAKSA

FRIED CARROT CAKE

A popular Peranakan dish, laksa comprises thick rice noodles steeped in a spicy gravy thickened with aromatic spices, shrimp paste and coconut milk. The tasty dish is often topped with thinly sliced cucumber, bean sprouts, fresh cockles, prawns and fish cakes, as well as sambal chilli and finely chopped laksa leaves.

Often mistaken to be an actual 'cake', fried carrot cake in Singapore is in fact made from radish steamed with rice flour. The resulting 'cake' is then stir fried and mixed with preserved radish (*chye poh*), eggs, chilli, diced garlic and spring onion. There are two popular variants: "black" with caramelised sweet black sauce and "white" with just the crispy fried egg charred to golden perfection.

ROJAK

MEE SIAM

Rojak is a savoury fruit and vegetable salad made from a medley of ingredients, including cucumber, turnip, pineapple, bean sprouts, grilled cuttlefish, crushed peanuts and fried dough sticks (*you char kueh*) all tossed in a flavourful dressing. This sticky dark sauce contains tamarind sauce, prawn paste, chilli and sugar. The result is an exquisite combination of savoury, sweet and sour flavours that is both delicious and refreshing.

Mee siam is a Malay speciality made of thin rice noodles fried with prawn paste and spices. Served with dried bean curd (*tau kwa*), boiled egg and paired with an aromatic, sweet and sour, salted soy bean gravy, this well-loved dish is garnished with spring onions and chinese chives.

DURIAN

SINGAPORE SLING

The pungent "king of fruits", as the durian is commonly known, is an acquired taste. The creamy golden flesh ensconced in a thorny husk has been described to taste like anything from a rich almond-flavoured custard to cream cheese and even the occasional wet rag. With its strong, distinctive odour, the durian is banned on all modes of public transport within Singapore.

The Singapore Sling is synonymous with the Raffles Hotel, where the popular cocktail is reputed to have been created in the early 1900s. A unique concoction containing gin, cherry brandy, pineapple juice, Cointreau and Grenadine, amongst others, the Singapore Sling is the main draw at the hotel's renowned Long Bar.

KUEH PIE TEE

TANG YUAN

A classic nyonya favourite, kueh pie tee are dainty, crispy pastry cups filled with stewed turnip and shredded bamboo shoots, and topped with a variety of ingredients such as succulent prawns, egg strips, fresh parsley and chilli.

Traditionally eaten during the 15th day of the Chinese New Year, tang yuan are glutinous rice balls cooked in a light ginger or peanut soup. Served plain or with delicious fillings such as red bean, peanut or sesame paste, the tang yuan's round shape symbolises family togetherness and as such, they are usually eaten together with one's family.

VADAI

PULUT HITAM

Vadai are a tasty South Indian snack made from ground lentils, dhal or diced potato, generously seasoned with onions, curry leaves, chilli and black mustard seeds. These deep-fried fritters are best eaten while still hot and crunchy, accompanied with coconut chutney and *sambar*, a vegetable stew based on a tamarind broth.

Usually eaten as a tea time treat, pulut hitam ('black rice' in Malay) is a sweet porridge made with black glutinous rice. This popular dessert is drizzled with fragrant coconut milk just before serving and sometimes topped with dried longan, a tropical fruit native to Southeast Asia.

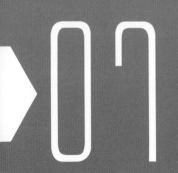

07

ATTRACTIONS

From the high-octane exhilaration of the world's first-ever Formula 1 night race to the majestic Integrated Resorts and Sentosa, Singapore's all-in-one entertainment and leisure hotspot, there's something for everyone from the young to the young-at-heart.

SENTOSA

Once a small fishing village just south of Singapore, Sentosa Island is today a bustling island resort with a myriad of entertainment and recreational facilities. Home to Resorts World Sentosa Integrated Resort and Southeast Asia's first Universal Studios theme park, as well as a smorgasbord of attractions from a dolphin lagoon to ZoukOut, the popular annual beachside dance festival, Sentosa is Singapore's quintessential must-visit destination.

sentosa

SENTOSA LUGE & SKYRIDE

Part go-cart, part toboggan, the Luge offers everyone from speed demons to casual riders an addictive rush of adrenaline as they whiz (or meander) down a 650-metre course ending at Silosa Beach. From there, the "ski-lift" Skyride transports both rider and cart back up the hill with a scenic treetop view of the city skyline.

RESORTS WORLD SENTOSA

One of Singapore's two Integrated Resorts, Resorts World Sentosa is a sprawling 49-hectare entertainment and leisure playground on Sentosa Island. Home to Universal Studios Singapore, six world-class hotels, a grand casino and an eclectic array of celebrity chef restaurants and brand-name boutiques, Resorts World Sentosa has something to offer everyone.

Contemporary design blends seamlessly with artistic flair at Hotel Michael, a tribute to renowned architect Michael Graves.

Crockfords Tower: An exclusive by-invitation-only luxury hotel with all-suite accommodation and extensive amenities.

UNIVERSAL STUDIOS

Blockbuster adventure comes to Southeast Asia with Universal Studios Singapore, the region's first Hollywood movie theme park.

THE JEWEL BOX

Reminiscent of a glittering jewel case from afar, the Jewel Box's epicurean gems are second only to its stunning views of the Singapore city and harbour. Nestled in the lush surrounds of tropical rainforest atop Mount Faber, the iconic hilltop destination is accessible via the stylish Jewel Cable Car, a cableway system linking Mount Faber and Sentosa Island.

MARINA BAY SANDS

An architectural marvel that has redefined Singapore's skyline, the landmark Marina Bay Sands Integrated Resort offers everything from a luxury hotel to state-of-the-art convention facilities, as well as an eclectic mix of retail boutiques and restaurants by celebrity chefs such as Daniel Boulud, Mario Batali, Tetsuya Wakuda and Guy Savoy. Taking pride of place at the top of the hotel towers is the Sands SkyPark, a sky oasis featuring lush greenery, gourmet dining options and an infinity pool overlooking the central business district.

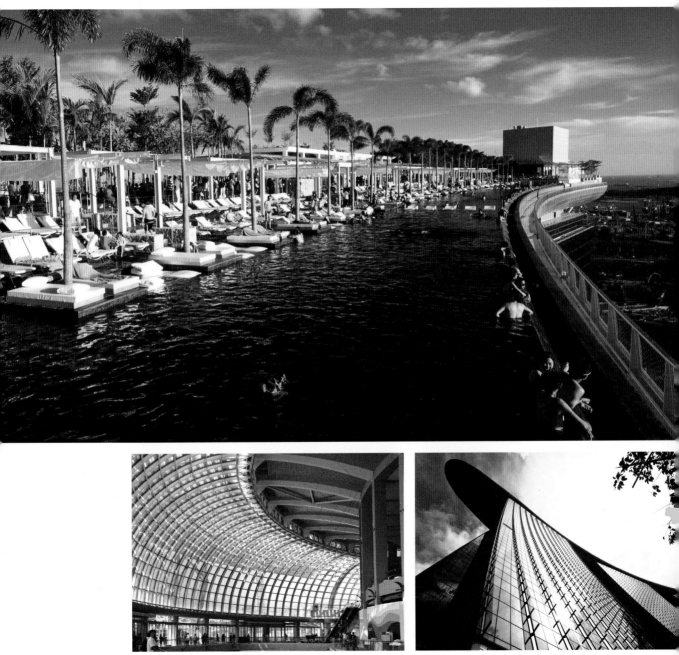

SINGAPORE FLYER

Strategically located in the heart of bustling Marina Bay, the 165-metre Singapore Flyer – the world's largest Giant Observation Wheel – offers an amazing 360-degree panoramic view of Singapore.

Visitors enjoy bird's-eye views of historical and cultural gems the likes of Chinatown, Sultan Mosque and Little India, as well as modern icons such as the Marina Barrage, Marina Bay Sands Integrated Resort and Central Business District.

Adrenaline aficionados and glamour
fashionistas alike look forward to each
September, when the world's only Formula 1
night race takes place at the transformed
Marina Bay Street Circuit. The annual event
ramps up the glamour, bright lights and high-
octane action from renowned Formula 1
drivers the likes of Fernando Alonso, Sebastian
Vettel and Lewis Hamilton.

FORMULA 1 SINGTEL SINGAPORE GRAND PRIX

The Singapore Central Business District undergoes a spectacular transformation each year in preparation for the world's only Formula 1 night race.

SINGAPORE ZOO

Over 3,000 animals have made their home at the Singapore Zoo, an open-concept rainforest zoo with spacious surroundings akin to their natural habitats. Marvel at the elephants of Asia and catch playful orang utans in the world's first free-ranging habitat, or have breakfast with the gentle primates at the award-winning "Jungle Breakfast with Wildlife" programme.

NIGHT SAFARI

As night falls, the day has just begun for over 1,000 nocturnal animals at the Night Safari. Embark on a fascinating journey through the world's first open-air wildlife night park, and spot animals such as lions, tarsiers and Indian rhinoceroses as they frolic and graze by the moonlight.

JURONG BIRD PARK

The largest bird park in the world, the Jurong Bird Park is a haven for 8,000 feathered friends from over 600 species. Watch with bated breath as majestic hawks, falcons and eagles perform stunning aerial manoeuvres in a simulated hunt in the popular Birds of Prey Show, and get up close and personal with over 1,500 free-flying birds in the world's largest walk-in African Waterfall Aviary.

PHOTO CREDITS

All photos by Bernard Go except as indicated below:

Bukit Timah Nature Reserve • East Coast Park •
MacRitchie Reservoir • Pulau Ubin • Southern Ridges •
Sungei Buloh Wetland Reserve
Photos courtesy of National Parks Board

Capella Singapore
Photos courtesy of Capella Singapore

Formula 1 Singtel Singapore Grand Prix
Photos courtesy of Singapore GP

Jurong Bird Park • Night Safari • Singapore Zoo
Photos courtesy of Wildlife Reserves Singapore

Klapsons The Boutique Hotel
Photos courtesy of klapsons, The Boutique Hotel

Marina Bay Sands
Photos courtesy of Marina Bay Sands Pte Ltd

Singapore Flyer
Photos courtesy of Singapore Flyer

The Jewel Box
Photos courtesy of Mount Faber Leisure Group Pte Ltd

Wanderlust
Photos courtesy of Wanderlust Hotel

OTHERS

Benjamin Yap: 42–43, 59, 60, 62 (left), 63,
    68 (bottom two)

Bernard Go: 79 (vertical three), 137 (right), 139 (right),
    159 (bottom left), 161 (bottom three, right)

Edward Hendricks: 28–31

Katong Antique House: 30 (Peranakan bridal couple)

Lin YangChen: 52

Marianne Rogerson: 115 (evolution garden), 120, 121
    (Southern Ridges), 125–126, 128–129, 130 (middle),
    131, 132 (wakeboard), 141, 171 (orang utan &
    tiger), 172 (bottom two),
    173 (leopard)

Marshall Cavendish Archives: 5 (food),
    10 (Vanda Miss Joachim), 18 (mooncakes), 136,
    137 (satay), 138, 139 (laksa), 140, 142–143

Rendo Yap: 26–27

Stephen Chong: 132 (barbecue)